THE MARTIAL METHOD

5 SYSTEMS
TO PROGRAM
YOUR LIFE

LEWIS E. BRIGGS

THE MARTIAL METHOD

Copyright © 2021 by LEWIS E. BRIGGS

All rights reserved. No part of this publication may be reproduced, distributed, or transmitted in any form or by any means, including photocopying, recording, or other electronic or mechanical methods, without the prior written permission of the publisher, except in the case of brief quotations embodied in critical reviews and certain other noncommercial uses permitted by copyright law.

武道

CONTENTS

CHAPTER 1 Life is Suffering 1
CHAPTER 2 The Three Rules 7
CHAPTER 3 The Five Hindrances 19
CHAPTER 4 Daily Mantra 77
CHAPTER 5 Sixteen Virtues of Achilleus 85
CHAPTER 6 Memento Mori 91
CHAPTER 7 Action 97

FURTHER READING 103
THANK YOU FOR YOUR TIME AND EFFORT 111

CHAPTER 1
Life is Suffering

This is the first maxim of the Buddha's Four Noble Truths. Or rather, he said something more like 'life is dukkha', which can best be translated as 'life is *unsatisfactory*'. This is not a nihilistic or negative outlook on life: it is a clear and direct observation of the human condition. You know this to be true from your own experience! If your life is perfect, if you have no complaints and do not wish for change, then I have nothing to teach you.

But I'm willing to bet that isn't the case. We're all contending with life, striving from one day to the next to keep our head above water and conquer the situation.

> *"To those human beings who are of any concern to me, I wish suffering, desolation, sickness, ill-treatment, indignities - I wish that they should not remain unfamiliar with profound self contempt, the torture of self mistrust... I have no pity for them, because I wish them the only thing that can prove today whether one is worth anything or not - that one endures."*
>
> **~ Friedrich Nietzsche**

The good news is, you're not the first person to encounter this problem. We have extensive records of great leaders, stretching back over thousands of years, who have mastered and overcome the exact same issues you're dealing with today. They were able to teach their methods to others, as I am now going to teach them to you. Just as they were able to completely revolutionise their lives, I am going to revolutionise yours.

Life is indeed suffering, we know this, and I understand that the specific nature of your individual problems are as wide and varied as there are infinite circumstances in the world. What I am going to give you are 5 universal systems, which will act as the foundation of your personal conduct. This is a playbook for you to refer to when you encounter the challenges you are bound to face in your everyday life, it will equip you with the right tools and mindset so that you are able to triumph over all obstacles.

THE MARTIAL METHOD

> *"I must create a system, or become part of some other man's."*
>
> **~ William Blake**

I did not know how to deal with anger when I was younger. I thought my negative emotions were excused by circumstance and other people's behaviour, and I was certain I could out-argue everyone with facts and reason. Despite my desire to achieve great things, I did not know how to motivate myself into action. The media portrays many heroes and provides us with people we are supposed to emulate, but I had no clear picture of exactly which virtues I should be making an effort to cultivate. Like most people, I feared death and had no idea how to accept my own mortality.

What I have now are Systems. I know exactly what problems I am going to face in life and precisely how I should engage with those issues. The Martial Method is a system I have developed in over a decade of experience. As a martial artist, a personal trainer, an Infantry Reservist, a psychonaut, a monk, as a husband, and soon as a father, I have lived an exciting life. During that time I have been fortunate enough to work with some of the very best. My teachers have been Thai champion muay thai fighters, world champion powerlifters, Infantry soldiers who were deployed in both Iraq and Afghanistan, monks at the head Soto Zen temple in Japan, and so many more. Along with an extensive library of literature from many of history's greatest minds, The Martial Method is a system I have created as the culmination of this wealth of experience.

> "It is circumstances which show men what they are. Therefore when a difficulty falls upon you, remember that God, like the trainer of wrestlers, has matched you with a rough young man. "For what purpose?" you may say. Why, that you may become an Olympic conqueror; but it is not accomplished without sweat."
>
> **~ Epictetus**

With over eight years of professional teaching experience, I have helped thousands of clients, students, and friends radically change the trajectory of their lives. I am confident in the effectiveness of this system, not only due to my own experience, but also from the results I've seen with my students in England, my country of birth, all the way to here in Japan, my country of residence.

A successful person is not a person without problems: a successful person is one who has learnt to deal with them. With these 5 systems I will give you the tools you need to confidently engage with the problems you face in life.

> "Excellence withers without an adversary: the time for us to see how great it is, how much its force, is when it displays its power through endurance. I assure you, good men should do the same: they should not be afraid to face hardships and difficulties, or complain of

> *fate; whatever happens, good men should take it in good part, and turn it to a good end; it is not what you endure that matters, but how you endure it."*
>
> **~ Seneca**

I do not know who you are, and I don't know your personal circumstances. But what I do know is that without a plan of attack, without a clearly defined system to engage the challenges you face in life, you're going to roll the dice on your own fate. It'll be anyone's guess if you're going to make it out alive!

With the Martial Method, you will be armed with the weapons you need to go on the offensive and take control of your own destiny.

> *"You are your own master, who else would be your master? Those who master themselves will cut all bondage."*
>
> **~ Dhammapada**

You don't need to worry about starting: you've already done that. In purchasing this book you've already made the conscious decision that you are on the journey toward becoming the person you want to be, and living the life you want to live.

Without further delay, let us begin with the three most important rules you need to live by, right now.

CHAPTER 2
The Three Rules

Rule #1: Breathe

Of all the things I could remove from you right now, what would kill you the fastest?
Air.

How long can you survive without breathing?
I can hold my breath for just 4 minutes. Aleix Segura set the world record at an incredible 24 minutes and 3 seconds.

The ability to breathe freely is something everyone takes for granted. But when it is taken away from you it immediately becomes your primary concern. Correction: your *only* concern.

Breathing is the most basic function of the human body, and oxygen is the most fundamental nutrient we consume. A newborn baby will take its first breath within ten seconds of being born, from that moment we don't stop breathing until we die. Considering the utmost importance of breathing, it's a wonder that so few people utilise the full capacity of their breath.

The research behind the benefits of breathwork is extensive and exhaustive, but the knowledge is not new. The vital importance of the breath and its relation to both body and mind dates back as far as recorded history. The Taoists of ancient China called this energy *qi*, and Hindus call it *prana* (one of the key concepts of yoga). A little later, in the West, the Greek term *pneuma* and the Hebrew term *rûah* referred to both the breath and the divine presence.

It wasn't until I was in my late 20s that I became fully aware of the critical importance of breathwork, and the profound ability it has to radically change our lives. I developed my own experience first through exercise; with long, consistent running and short, explosive powerlifting being opposite ends of the spectrum, and martial combat somewhere in between. Also through yoga, in which the bond of movement and breath is paramount, then with meditation, in which penetrating focus and awareness of the breath allows us to deepen and extend it more than you would think possible. And finally, with the increasingly popular Wim Hof technique, which is similar to the ancient Tummo breathing practices of Tibetan Buddhists.

There is no one-size-fits-all method of breathing. The type and technique of breathing we must employ varies drastically depending on the situation, and the activity we are engaged with.

But to begin, let me give you a basic method for you to employ first, as a general-purpose response to most normal conditions.

First: inhale deeply through the nose.

Second: exhale long and smoothly through either the nose or mouth; whichever you feel is most comfortable.

On the inhalation, breathe down, deep into the tanden (the part of your core a couple of inches below the navel). Try to avoid breathing into the chest, but instead all the way down into the stomach. This will engage the diaphragm, which is much stronger than the intercostal muscles between the ribs. Breathing with the diaphragm also activates the vagus nerve, engaging the parasympathetic nervous system, which helps with relaxation, lowering heart rate, easing hypertension and aiding digestion.

To practice diaphragmatic breathing specifically: lie flat on your back and place one hand on your chest, and the other on your stomach. Now breathe without moving your chest, instead creating as much movement as possible down in your stomach.

On the exhalation we want it to be long and smooth, but we also want to keep it comfortable and easy. Don't force it too much, the more unnatural it is the more difficult it will be to adopt it as our instinctive mode of breathing.

On the outward breath: breathe easily, but at the end of the breath just add a little 20% extra. Like you are adding an extra sigh of comfort on the end, the type of breath you might let out after you throw yourself into a large, freshly made bed.

With this gentle extension of the exhalation, you can comfortably lengthen your breath in a way that will slowly become your natural mode of breathing.

Deep inhale.
Long exhale.

> *"Lord Sanenori said, "In the midst of a single breath, where perversity cannot be held, is the Way." If so, then the Way is one. But there is no one who can understand this clarity at first. Purity is something that cannot be attained except by piling effort upon effort."*
>
> **~ Yamamoto Tsunetomo**

With this you have begun to breathe consciously, and thus live intentionally.

This exercise is also the fundamental practice of meditation; which we will discuss in more detail, later in the book.

> *"Chale vāte chalaṃ chittaṃ niśchale niśchalaṃ bhavet*
> *Yoghī sthāṇutvamāpnoti tato vāyuṃ nirodhayet*
> *When the breath wanders the mind is unsteady. But when the breath is calmed, the mind too will be still."*
>
> **~ Yogi Svātmārāma**

Rule #2: Hydrate

You can survive without air for a matter of minutes. You can survive without water for a matter of days.

Water is life. All living organisms were born from it, and must consume it to continue existing.

Dehydration can lead to or exacerbate a variety of problems, such as; cardiovascular disease, arthritis, kidney failure, depression, anxiety, memory loss, headaches and physical fatigue, to name just a few.

I had the value of water drilled into me in the Army. During my time as an Infantry Reservist the British Army had been involved in the Afghan war for over 12 years, fighting in some of the hottest and most arid environments in the world. It was constantly drilled into us that our two most important resources were water and ammunition.

If you get thirsty, you're already dehydrated.

There is no universally agreed upon amount of water that we should be drinking within a day. This varies depending on body composition, environment and activity, as well as many other factors. A good place to start is a bare minimum of 2 litres of water per day, and then aim for 4 litres or more.

Does 4 litres of straight water sound like a lot to drink in a single day? Think about how much alcohol you can drink in a single night. 4 litres is 7 pints in the UK (8.5 US). I'd be willing to bet that most men have drunk more than that in the space of a few hours.

So what's the benefit of drinking all this H2O?
To start with, water promotes cardiovascular health. Blood is more than 90% water. Dehydration lowers the volume of your blood, so your heart must work harder to pump the reduced amount and get enough oxygen to your cells.

Water also keeps you cool: Your body releases heat by expanding blood vessels close to the skin's surface (this is why your face gets red during exercise), resulting in more blood flow and more heat dissipating into the air. When you're dehydrated however, it takes a higher environmental temperature to trigger blood vessels to widen, meaning you stay hotter for longer.

Hydration significantly affects energy levels and brain function. Studies show that even mild dehydration, such as the loss of 1-3% of body weight, can impair many aspects of brain function. In a study of young men and women, researchers found that fluid loss of 1.5% after exercise impaired both mood and concentration, and was also detrimental to working memory and increased feelings of anxiety and fatigue. It also increased the frequency of headaches.

You can easily measure how much fluid you have lost through perspiration by weighing yourself before and after exercise, which is especially important whilst training in hot summer months. "For every pound of sweat you lose, that's a pint of water you'll need to replenish." says John Batson M.D, a sports medicine physician, adding that it's not unusual for a high school football player to lose 5 pounds or more of sweat during summer practice.

I understand that drinking pure, unflavoured water can be challenging for some people; especially if you're used to drinking tea, coffee, juice, or god forbid carbonated softdrinks.

It didn't start to feel completely natural for me until I made it an explicit part of my morning routine. The second task of my morning routine, immediately after I have woken up, is to pour myself a glass of water, which I finish drinking by the end of my routine. Beginning every single day with a tall glass of water has completely changed my mindset toward drinking straight water. Now, when I am offered a selection of drinks by friends or family, I usually opt for plain water, out of genuine preference.

Can you guess what the first task of my daily routine is?
To step outside and take three deep breaths.
Don't forget Rule #1!

A specifically formulated morning routine is one of the most powerful practices we can apply, guaranteed to frame our day correctly and set us off on the right foot every time.

The key to drinking sufficient water throughout the day is to have it available at all times. Where ever you are, whether you're busy at home, sat at a desk in the office, or on the move between locations, you should have a drink of water within arms reach. Don't wait until you're thirsty to go and get water. Have it there, ready immediately.

Stay hydrated, stay alive.

Rule #3: Posture

Sit up straight.

Don't slouch:
If you're leaning against the back of a chair, push your hips back as far as they will go and straighten your lower back. Draw your shoulders back and down, and let your head float up toward the ceiling as if it's a balloon on the end of a string.

The benefits of correct posture are life changing. Sitting or standing up straight has a direct affect on your breathing, digestion and the health of your muscles and joints. Your posture is also a critical component of your non-verbal body language, which has a huge influence on how other people think and feel about you, as well as governing how you think and feel about yourself.

To start with (rule #1!) slouching shortens the muscles in your anterior chain, along the front of your body, constricting your ribs and stomach, which reduces oxygen intake by as much as 30%. You already know how important it is to breathe deep, and it's nearly impossible to take a full breath in a slouched position, so sit up straight.

When you have good posture your internal organs align well; meaning less compression on your stomach, intestines and liver, which facilitates the free flow of food and digestive juices. A slouched posture inhibits the normal activity of the gastrointestinal system, which makes you vulnerable to digestive distress, including constipation and acid reflux.

Your body is designed to stand in a 'neutral' position in which the pelvis, head and torso are vertically aligned. Forward head, tilted hips, or an overly curved spine puts stress on muscles in ways they aren't designed to endure. Over the long term, this stress causes pain - usually in the back. When you have good posture you use the muscles that support your spine properly. Standing and sitting with good posture uses your muscles in the way they were designed, so your body - especially your back - feels better for longer.

Your posture not only affects you physiologically, but also has an incredible psychological impact on your life. Social psychologist Amy Cuddy tested two groups of people, in which she asked participants to sit or stand in power-poses for just two minutes, taking swab samples before and after the exercise. Participants who adopted dominant, high-power poses showed a 20% increase in testosterone, a 25% decrease in cortisol, and 86% of the group were likely to gamble at the end of the exercise. Whereas test subjects who adopted more submissive, low-power poses showed a 10% decrease in testosterone, 15% increase in cortisol, and 60% of the group were likely to gamble when asked. A remarkable difference for simply engaging a powerful posture for two short minutes.

People who sit and stand with good posture are more likely to be judged as more competent, enthusiastic and confident, as well as more approachable, charismatic and attractive. The vital benefits of this assessment are easy to imagine. In a professional setting good posture can easily mean the difference between getting hired or promoted. Socially, it can make the difference between your future spouse looking twice in your direction, or ignoring your presence entirely.

Your body influences your mind, your mind changes your behaviour, and your behaviour predicts your outcome.

In Buddhism it is said that there are four postures:

- Lying
- Sitting
- Standing
- Walking

At almost all times you are in some variation of these postures. No matter what action you engage in, whether you are extremely busy or even completely asleep, you remain in one of these four postures. Posture, along with breathing, are the two fundamental attributes of every individual's current experience. You can stop whatever you are doing, cease all action, but no matter how much you rid yourself of activity, you will always continue to breathe, and will always continue to exist in one of the four postures.

> *"To sit in meditation, you must be like a general on horseback in front of his army."*
>
> **~ Taisen Deshimaru**

Tall, straight, and in control. But not stiff or uncomfortable. Firm yet relaxed, confident and easy. For most people it will take concerted effort at first, simply because it is something they are not familiar with. We have such comfy sofas, office chairs and car seats, it is so easy to spend 99% of our day completely disengaged. We are not really sitting in these chairs, we're lying down while they prop us up! Sitting up tall and unsupported, with a straight back, is how we sat for hundreds of thousands of years before the industrial era bestowed upon us the gifts of leather sofas and swivel chairs.

Sitting, standing, walking and lying with correct posture may take a while to get used to, but I promise you, it will become comfortable and easy, and when it does, you will thank me, and yourself, for the rest of your life!

These are the three rules. They apply to everyone, at all times. Remember them well, so that you are able to recall them under any circumstance, and hold yourself in accordance with them at all times.

#1 - Breathe
#2 - Hydrate
#3 - Posture

Master these fundamental rules before you move onto the next steps. If you think they are 'basic', this is only because they are so foundational to your entire life. If you think they are 'easy', then I expect you to be able to stay on top of these principles throughout the entire day, every day.

When you are ready for the next step, we will discuss the five main obstacles which challenge us and create difficulty within our lives. I guarantee you have faced all of these problems already, and will certainly experience them again. In the following chapter, we will identify these hindrances and provide a system of clear, direct solutions to remedy the situation.

CHAPTER 3
The Five Hindrances

Desire

It has been said that all suffering is the result of unfulfilled desire. When we speak of desire we often talk about the grasping mentality; the wanting and craving for things and experiences. You must remember that the rejecting mind is also desire. When you want something to be other than it is, you experience desire - desire for change - and that is when you suffer.

Of course that is not to say that it is wrong to want anything, nor is it to say that these desires should be rejected entirely, but the nature in which you experience desire should be studied closely.

We live in a hedonistic age of abundance in which everyone is addicted to something. Desire for sensory pleasure should be proportional and not over-indulged in, as it serves little or no benefit to the individual beyond immediate gratification.

To satisfy your cravings and indulge your senses is certainly pleasurable, but pleasure is of fleeting value.
The gratification found from satisfying your desire for pleasure is temporary. True, lasting happiness can only be discovered within deep contentment.

> "No desire is serenity
> And the world settles of itself."
>
> **~ Lao Tzu, Tao Te Ching**

The first step toward overcoming desire is to recognise it. Recognise the feeling of desire when it arises. If you consciously disassociate yourself from the emotion you can prevent it from controlling your thoughts and actions. Realise that your feelings and desires are something external, and that your current experience is not an intrinsic part of your being.
Stop for a moment and simply examine the feeling of desire as it arises, sometimes this is all it takes to weaken its power and influence, and allow you to consciously overcome it.

However, when that's not enough, there are two further systems you can employ to dispel the hindrance of desire.

Discipline

Discipline is nothing more than the ability for you to obey your own commands, regardless of how you feel.

Discipline is extremely important to everyone in all walks of life, but especially to a Warrior practicing the Martial Method. Discipline reflects desire in the form of self-restraint and temperance. This is a key virtue we are going to discuss at length, so let's take a deep dive into discipline and make sure we understand exactly what it is, before we learn how to utilize it.

> "In the constitution of the rational being I can see no virtue that counters justice: but I do see the counter to pleasure - self-control."
>
> **~ Marcus Aurelius**

To many people, discipline is a dirty word. To some it conjures images of punishment and suffering. While discipline is sometimes applied as a form of corrective punishment, the key to understanding discipline is that it is something which is instilled *within yourself.*

> **The Oxford definition of discipline reads:**
>
> *"The practice of training people to obey rules or a code of behaviour, using punishment to correct disobedience."*

In both the military and martial arts discipline is instilled in people so that they will obey a set of rules or code of behaviour under their own supervision.

Let me give you a clear example:
Among the civilian population there is an idea of the Army; of drill instructors and scary sergeants screaming at enlisted men all the time. But in reality, this kind of behaviour is almost entirely reserved for training. Whilst in training you may be punished to correct your mistakes and disobedience, ensuring that in the future you will obey the rules and code of behaviour, as expected of you within the Armed Forces. Does that sound familiar? Read the Oxford definition again.

As a recruit you are subjected to this form of discipline so that while on deployment you don't need to be told what to do. When you're deployed in the field, your superior officers and non-commissioned officers (NCOs) do not have time to be holding your hand. You need to be trusted to act without constant supervision, often in the most challenging of circumstances.

When your mistake is being corrected with punishment during training, that is the act of discipline being applied to you. What it creates within you, is the quality of discipline.

> *"Perhaps the most valuable result of all education is the ability to make yourself do the thing you have to do when it ought to be done, whether you like it or not."*
>
> **~ Thomas Huxley**

We have all experienced different lives; with different parents, teachers, friends and circumstances which have led us to this point. Whatever level of discipline you maintain right now, that's fine. Whether you consider your own discipline to be weak, or if you have the steadfast resolve of a seasoned warrior, we can all progress and develop our discipline further.

Some people believe their mental traits are fixed, that 'we are who we are'. I believe this to be false.

We can develop our discipline, as with any aspect of ourselves. It only requires the application of time and effort.

Here are three techniques to reinforce your discipline, and develop your self-control to the level of a warrior monk.

#1 Find a Strong Reason Why

A strong reason for action is an external factor, related to *motivation*, which is a key topic we will discuss in more detail later.

For now, I want you to consider how having a truly great reason for your actions can help to develop discipline within you.

For many people, having a child completely changes their work ethic, for others, the reason could be paying medical bills for a sick relative. External factors like these give us huge motivation and drive to accomplish our goals. These are the sort of conditions that get you out of bed in the morning and keep you going, even when you're burned out.

This habit applied over time becomes discipline, and will solidify itself into your code of ethics.

#2 Routine

> *"There is no more miserable human being, than the one for whom the beginning of every bit of work must be decided anew each day."*
>
> **~ William James**

Routine is a factor I sometimes struggle with. As I have spent almost my entire adult life self-employed, I often have a wildly irregular schedule.

When we are able to build a routine and adhere to a predictable schedule, we can accomplish anything with greater ease and regularity.

In the Army I had to wake up around 4:30 every day, which for me was super early, but once I had been getting up on time every day for a couple of weeks, it became surprisingly easy.
At the start of basic training, the alarm went off and I dragged myself out of bed like a zombie, but after a couple of weeks I woke up naturally *before* the alarm.

Develop a morning routine. If you don't have a morning routine, one will be assigned to you.

Whether we're aware of it or not, we all have a routine. You must consciously curate your own routine and apply effort to develop something beneficial, that you can maintain over time until it entrenches itself within you, and when it does, you will have become more disciplined.

#3 If-Then Technique

Originally called 'implementation intention', this concept was created by psychologist Peter Gollwitzer in the 90s. With this technique you are able to prepare yourself for anything that may challenge your discipline; any temptation or obstacles you predict you may encounter beforehand.

For example, let's say that you are trying to save money, and want to cut back on your expenses.

If you go on Amazon, **then** you will only buy the essentials you need for home or work.

Or **if** you go out for a drink with friends, **then** you will only have one drink before going home.

It is much easier to stick to what you have planned, than it is to restrain yourself in the heat of the moment.

With this technique you are able to prepare yourself for some of the temptations you expect to face, so when you do encounter them you can default to these preset responses without having to consciously engage yourself and make any tough decisions.

That is exactly what the Martial Method is about: proven procedures and systems, preparing yourself for any eventuality.

On the path to overcoming desire you must rely on discipline. Engage these three practices to strengthen yours:

#1 - Find a Strong Reason Why

#2 - Routine

#3 - If-Then Technique

With these three techniques you will be able to develop your discipline, which is always your first and greatest weapon in the battle against desire.

Every time you experience desire it becomes a test of discipline. If you choose to give in and indulge yourself, you will strengthen that desire. However, every time you make the choice to abstain and resist your desires, you maintain and strengthen your discipline.

Aparigraha

In Hinduism and Jainism, aparigraha is the virtue of non-possessiveness and non-grasping, and refers to keeping the desire for possessions to what is necessary or important.

> *"Yamaoka Tesshu owned only three tatami mats in his house, one for meditation, one for guests and one for his wife and himself."*

To live the life of a Warrior Monk, you needn't reject all possessions and live a completely ascetic lifestyle. We practice the Middle Way, a life of neither complete indulgence nor extreme austerity.

Of course, it is up to your own personal judgement to decide what could be considered 'necessary' or 'important'. But if you keep the moderate nature of aparigraha in mind it will aid you in combating the seductive nature of desire, and alleviate the burden of the first hindrance.

Take a break here. Before you move onto the second hindrance you need to digest and apply what you have learnt.

Consider how firm your discipline is, and apply the three techniques to develop your discipline further.

Recognition leads to mindfulness. Counteract desire with discipline. To cultivate discipline, apply the following:

#1 - Strong Reason Why
#2 - Routine
#3 - If-Then Technique

Always remember the mindset of aparigraha.

Anger

The second hindrance you must prepare yourself for is anger. Anger is a strong manifestation of rejection, but even the more subtle feelings of aversion or annoyance are types of anger.

Anger is an especially persuasive emotion, as you will often feel the most justified in experiencing it. If you believe you have been wronged in some way, that you are the victim of an injustice, you will quickly create a narrative in which you are entitled to your own anger.

It has been said that anger is a curse foremost to ourselves. Consider this: when you become angry, often the person you are angry at is not even aware of your feelings! Even with all the justification in the world, anger remains to be an insidious emotion, which will almost always leave you worse off than had you not indulged in it at all.

As a teenager, contempt and resentment were two of the primary hindrances I faced in my life, and emotions I projected on a daily basis. But now, thanks to the systems I have in place, I am able to recognize my feelings clearly and move beyond these emotions, into an entirely new world free from stress caused by my own anger.

If anger - or any kind of rejection - is a feeling you struggle with often, get ready to take some notes; the following methods will change your life.

There are two forms of anger I will teach you how to deal with. Anger which is caused by an external source, and anger which manifests internally.

The first involves confrontation and discord we receive from others, the second includes the emotional content that arises and originates from within ourselves.

His Nature, My Judgement, Direct Pointing

> *"Father, forgive them; for they know not what they do."*
>
> **~ Luke 23:34**

It is said that to know all, is to forgive all. No one wants to be angry. Anger arises from a state of unconsciousness. If you are conscious of this fact and aware of the circumstances affecting the people involved, it is possible for you to choose another path, a path of clarity and stillness, even when being directly subjected to the aggression and anger of others.

The first system I will share with you is something I created with the help of two friends: Marcus Aurelius and a man that we'll call Frank

Marcus Aurelius was a Roman Emperor, a Stoic philosopher, and one of the greatest leaders mankind has ever seen. My number one book recommendation, and one of my own sacred texts, is that of Marcus Aurelius' Meditations.
Frank was a housemate I lived with with in the UK before leaving for Japan.

Fortunately, I began studying Stoic philosophy as I lived with Frank, and I needed it. Because Frank is, without a shadow of a doubt, the angriest person I have ever encountered in my life.

Never, before or since, have I encountered anyone so permanently full of rage that they are constantly on the verge of flying into a fit of anger.

As I lived with Frank I also began working in security, bouncing doors at bars and nightclubs on the weekend. So not only did I apply this three step system to Frank, but also to drunk, angry punters in a professional environment.

Whether you are engaging the anger of a bully you meet every day, at school, in the workplace, among family and friends, or if it is a chance encounter on the street with someone you will never see again, apply this system universally to overcome every situation.

#1 His Nature

> *"Whenever you meet someone, ask yourself first this immediate question: 'What beliefs does this person hold about the good and bad in life?' Because if he believes this or that about pleasure and pain and their constituents, about fame and obscurity, death and life, then I shall not find it surprising or strange if he acts in this or that way, and I shall remember that he has no choice but to act as he does."*
>
> **~ Marcus Aurelius**

Whenever you encounter a difficult person, the first thing you must do is consider the nature of this individual. If it's a person

THE MARTIAL METHOD

you are meeting for the first time, you won't have any prior knowledge of their character, but if it's someone you interact with often, you can think about your history with them, and what that tells you about the depths of their mindset.

When you are speaking with a person who often reacts in a confrontational way, it should not surprise you when they start getting angry. If you are dealing with the type of person who often has a jealous or spiteful mindset, again, you should not be surprised when they are led to behave as such.

Once you have seen the regular behaviour of a person, when you have gained some insight into their typical mode of operation, it should not surprise you when you see them act within the nature of their character.

> *"Say to yourself first thing in the morning: today I shall meet people who are meddling, ungrateful, aggressive, treacherous, malicious, unsocial. All this has afflicted them through their ignorance of true good and evil. But I have seen that the nature of good is what is right, and the nature of evil what is wrong; and I have reflected that the nature of the offender himself is akin to my own - not a kinship of blood or seed, but a sharing in the same mind, the same fragment of divinity. Therefore I cannot be harmed by any of them, as none will infect me with their wrong. Nor can I be angry with my kinsman or hate him. We were born for cooperation, like feet, like hands, like eyelids, like the*

> *rows of upper and lower teeth. So to work in opposition of one another is to work against nature: and anger or opposition is rejection."*
>
> **~ Marcus Aurelius**

Let me ask you, would it be reasonable to demand that you never meet an angry or confrontational person for the rest of your life?

Of course not. You know that the world is full of these people; this is a natural part of the human condition, the capacity for such behaviour exists within each of us as much as anyone else. You know that you will certainly encounter angry people many times throughout the rest of your life, don't act shocked when it happens, you knew this time would come!

> *"When you complain of the negative actions of another, turn inwards on yourself. The fault is clearly your own, for not expecting such a person to act in their nature."*
>
> **~ Marcus Aurelius**

As surely as the seasons change and the sun will rise, so long as we live in a community surrounded by other human beings, we will eventually encounter the anger, spitefulness, resentment and aggression of other people.

> *"Interactions with people are the major source of emotional turmoil, but it doesn't have to be that way. The problem is that we are continually judging people, wishing that they were something that they are not... We want them to think and act in a certain way, most often the way we think and act. And because this is not possible, because everyone is different, we are continually frustrated and upset. Instead, see other people as phenomena, as neutral as comets or plants. They simply exist... Work with what they give you, instead of resisting and trying to change them. Make understanding people a fun game, the solving of puzzles. It is all part of the human comedy."*
>
> **~Robert Greene**

Now we understand that these people are only acting within their nature. That's fine, but it is still damn annoying, right? I feel your pain, but don't worry: that's where step two comes into play.

#2 **My Judgement**

> *"Things cannot touch the mind: they are external and inert; anxieties can only come from your internal judgement."*
>
> **~ Marcus Aurelius**

'All is as thinking makes it so.'
If there is one maxim to live by, this is it.

This person causing you grief; if you think they are a problem, you are correct, they are a problem. If you think they are not a problem, you are also correct, they are not a problem.

You are only able to indirectly influence your surroundings. Despite the actions you take and the effort you apply, the results are not always exactly as you wish. You do, however, have complete control over your own judgement. No one is able to reach inside your mind and make you think or feel anything: you have complete intellectual sovereignty. No one can make you angry: you choose to allow circumstances to make you angry.

> *"No thief can steal your will."*
> **~ Epictetus**

As I work in security I regularly face angry, excited or scared people; men and women who have completely lost their composure. But I do not allow them to frame the situation with their emotional reaction. My judgement is my own, I maintain my center and mental clarity regardless of their influence.

> *"Harm to you cannot subsist in another's directing mind, nor indeed in any turn or change of circumstance. Where, then? In that part of you which judges harm. So no such judgement, and all is well."*
> **~Marcus Aurelius**

And so, we encounter an angry person.

Step 1: His Nature.

I understand that this person is acting within their nature, and I would be foolish to expect them to behave otherwise.

Step 2: My Judgement

I maintain my composure, and do not allow their words or actions to influence my own state of mind.

Once you have policed your own reaction and are able to remain serene in the face of their anger, your natural inclination may be to reach out and attempt to guide this person toward their own peace of mind, especially if it is someone you have to deal with often.

Do not forget, these angry people you meet, annoying though they may be, they themselves are the greatest victim of their own negativity and frustration. You are able to remove yourself from their presence, but they are not able to escape themselves: their torment is endless!

Whether you wish to help that person for their benefit or for your own is not important, however there is one very important fact you need to remember:

Most people hate being told what to do, especially if the advice is unsolicited.

I am a personal trainer. I work professionally as a teacher and instructor, I host a podcast, I regularly post on Twitter, and have published a book. My entire career revolves around telling people what to do, or at the very least sharing my thoughts and experience with them.

But what I do not do is stand on my soapbox on a street corner with a megaphone shouting to the mob. I only share what I know with people who have a genuine desire to learn.

The only time I will intervene and give unsolicited advice is when someone is a danger to either themselves, or to others.

If you lecture someone who doesn't want to know, the best you can hope for is that they will ignore you, the worst that can happen is that it will drive them even deeper into their wrongful behaviour.

How do you guide someone toward the light?

#3 Direct Pointing

You are only able to highlight the wrongdoing of another person through your own positive action. Be the change you wish to see in the world.

Imagine twins separated at birth. One is sent to a faraway temple to be raised by monks, the other to a prison to be raised by convicted criminals. How would those two children develop differently? What kind of people would they become?

This is the power of association, and the karmic effect each person has on their environment.

> *"You cannot teach a man anything; you can only help him to find it within himself."*
>
> **~ Galileo**

In exactly the same way that no one is able to reach inside your mind and force you to think a certain way, you are not able to reach inside the mind of anyone else and directly manipulate their behaviour.

You are, however, able to change the environment itself through your own words and actions.

This change will not happen overnight, and depending on the strength of their negativity you may not be able to penetrate their mindset at all. Short of physical intervention, the only course of action we have to take is to be the antidote to their poison.

- When they act with anger, you express compassion.
- When they behave jealously, you respond with generosity.
- When they are defensive of their ego, you are entirely without self.

> *"If a man's heart is rankling with discord and ill feeling toward you, you can't win him to your way of thinking with all the logic in Christendom. People don't want to change their minds. They can't be forced or driven to*

> *agree with you or me. But they may possibly be led to, if we are gentle and friendly, ever so gentle and ever so friendly."*
>
> **~ Abraham Lincoln**

This is not to say you should lie down and submit yourself to their aggression without resistance.

Set your own personal boundaries, make them clear and defend them as required.

What I am talking about is your mental response; about maintaining your intellectual and spiritual sovereignty. Most people are very emotional creatures; do not let their unconscious behaviour influence your reaction. Police your response and lead by example.

> *"Someone despises me? That is his concern. But I will see to it that I am not found guilty of any word or action deserving contempt. Will he hate me? That is his concern. But I will be kind and well-intentioned to all, and ready to show this very person what he is failing to see - not in any criticism or display of tolerance, but with genuine good will."*
>
> **~ Marcus Aurelius**

When encountering the negative actions of another, remind yourself first, that this person is only acting *within their nature* and you would be unreasonable to ask that such people not exist.

Second, that no one can reach in and manipulate your directing mind: *all judgements are your own*, disregard this judgement and all is well.

Last, *direct pointing*: highlight their wrongdoing not through criticism or lecture, but through your own positive actions.

Now you have controlled your immediate response to the anger of others, how do you deal with later frustration and lingering resentment?

Forgiveness, Compassion, Understanding

> *If I love myself despite my infinite faults, how can I hate anyone at the glimpse of a few faults?"*
>
> **~ Swamy Vivekananda**

As with desire, your first line of defence against the hindrance of anger is recognition. Especially with minor annoyances, simply being conscious of the feeling of anger as it arises within you can be enough to loosen its grip and free yourself of any reaction.

When you experience anger in the comfort of your own home, however, and cannot seem to shake lingering feelings of frustration and rejection, you must go further to consider the antidote to this negativity.

#1 Forgiveness

Forgiveness is an immediately calming response; even if you are a genuine victim of wrongdoing and free of responsibility, to hold onto anger will not change the past. In fact, to hold onto anger prolongs your own suffering, as you carry the condition with you.

> *"The weak can never forgive. Forgiveness is the attribute of the strong."*
>
> **~ Mahatma Gandhi**

To forgive a person does not mean to excuse or condone their actions; only to release yourself from feelings of anger or resentment. In this way, forgiveness is an emotion you extend to yourself as much as anyone else, much like anger itself.

Search deep within yourself and cultivate forgiveness. This virtue will become a wellspring of healing, and a key attribute in your battle against anger.

#2 Compassion

Compassion is a powerful force, especially when you feel anger toward someone you sincerely care about. At this time, you must remember your usual feelings toward them, and attempt to return yourself to a compassionate disposition.

All men are brothers, and live to the same end.

Compassion for all living beings is the highest ideal; the moral paradigm we must strive toward. To wish for anything else is to forget the universal nature of all humanity.

Forgiveness and compassion are thoughts easily extended to people you feel favourably toward. However, there are many people in the world you simply have no time for. For them, forgiveness or compassion may be too difficult to imagine, and that's when we need...

#3 Understanding

You should be able to understand everyone you encounter, whether you are particularly fond of them or not.

Everything arises from conditions, and everyone behaves the way they do based on their conditioned responses, developed from their own unique life experience.

No matter how vehemently you disagree with someone, you are only able to disagree with them if you first understand them. If you do not at the very least understand them, you cannot disagree with them: what you share is simply a misunderstanding.

When you understand the other person, you are far more likely to be able to find some common ground and resolve your differences amicably. If not, at least when you understand your opponent you will be better equipped to deal with them.

Endeavour always to see clearly and understand what motivates other people's thoughts and actions.

Further practice:

During meditation, apply the three stages of forgiveness, compassion and understanding. Apply them first to those you love: the people closest in your life. Then, extend the three stages to those a little further out: your close friends and trusted allies. Next, try to give the same consideration to people you feel neutral toward: work colleagues or acquaintances. Then apply the method to people you actively dislike, and even feel resentment toward. Finally, direct this consideration toward the people you feel the greatest anger toward.

If you go directly to the end and apply forgiveness, compassion and understanding to people you really can't stand, you will usually find that it does not work; you may be unable to overcome your initial feelings of rejection. When you begin with the people you love, on the other hand, it is as if dipping your toes slowly into water, allowing yourself to acclimatise and adjust to the right mindset, before working your way down the slope and submerging yourself fully in the three virtues.

Remember well, in the heat of the moment when facing external confrontation: *His Nature, My Judgement, Direct Pointing.*

In your own time, when you have an opportunity to reflect on your internal resistance: *Forgiveness, Compassion, Understanding.*

Laziness

What is laziness, but simply an unwillingness to work or use energy? Feelings of laziness exist within the mind as an aversion to effort, and a desire for comfort and the path of least resistance. The body reflects laziness in the sensation of sluggishness and lethargy.

However real the physiological effects of fatigue may be, we must not allow ourselves to become the experience. Effort must be made to maintain our directing mind as a reliable center of judgement.

Resistance manifests itself within us as procrastination. We experience this when we have intention and desire, but deep within our subconscious we remain unwilling.

> *"What is endeavour? It is finding joy in doing what is good. To do that, it is necessary to remove anything that counteracts it, especially laziness. Laziness has three aspects: having no wish to do good, being distracted by negative activities, and underestimating oneself by doubting one's ability. Related to these are taking undue pleasure in idleness and sleep and being indifferent to samsāra as a state of suffering."*
>
> **~ 13th Dalai Lama**

As always, recognition leads to mindfulness. Rather than associating ourselves with the feelings and causes of laziness, we recognize the emotions and physical sensations when they arise with impartial clarity, and engage ourselves consciously in affirmative action, regardless of how we feel about it.

But let's not stop there, I am giving you two keys to unlock the shackles of laziness: Discipline and Motivation.

Discipline

Again? We've been here before!

Absolutely right. It could be said that sufficient discipline is the answer to all your problems, but life's not that easy, for this reason I am giving you other options. Discipline is a particularly strong antidote to both desire and laziness, so we're going to return to it now and discuss one more tip to uncover the steadfast Warrior buried within.

Discipline reflects laziness in the form of self-motivation and drive. Remember the three techniques we discussed previously in our practice of developing discipline.

#1 - Strong Reason Why
#2 - Routine
#3 - If-Then Technique

You can employ these three techniques yourself, without the need for help from anyone else. But discipline is most easily instilled within you when it is applied by another person.

#4 Find a Teacher

The guru-shishya tradition of master and disciple was once held sacred as a foundation of common society. Now, there seems to be a low bar of entry to becoming a teacher, and the profession is mostly disregarded as a plain necessity and uninspired requirement of a bureaucratic education process.

However, there are many great teachers among us, not only professionally qualified tutors and instructors, but anyone you can learn from either directly or indirectly can fill the role of guru in your life.

It is much easier for another person to enforce discipline within you. As we discussed on the topic of desire, to apply discipline requires a certain amount of punishment and correction of your mistakes. It is of course much easier for another person to punish you, than it is for you to punish yourself.

If you're still a youngster and live with your parents, when they tell you to clean your room, or your school teachers expect you to complete your homework, don't kick up a stink: recognise this as an opportunity to develop discipline. The same principle applies to all ages. Whether you're dealing with your boss or any kind of instructor, turn up to work early, listen to what you're being told, don't just hear the words: apply them.

I get this from my wife now. Sometimes she asks me to do something I don't really want to do, but I know she's right, it might be a tedious or unpleasant task, but it's a job that needs doing. So rather than feeling like she's nagging me and resenting her for the inconvenience, I thank her for the incentive. Thank you for the motivation, Airi. Thank you for helping to guide me on the path of discipline.

You don't have to wait for these people to come to you: you can seek out teachers and actively ask for help. Make yourself accountable. If you're trying to quit smoking and are really serious about it, tell your friends, give them complete discretion to slap you across the face if they see you touch a cigarette.
If you have good friends, and you honestly, sincerely ask them, impressing upon them the seriousness of your conviction, they will hold you to that commitment.

To recognise quality teachers, and to capitalise on the lessons you learn from them requires a paramount shift in mindset. You absolutely must move from a *fixed*, to a *growth mindset*.

Fixed mindset

A fixed mindset is extremely limiting. When you have a fixed mindset, you believe that your qualities and traits, such as practical abilities and intelligence, are static and cannot be improved upon. People with a fixed mindset generally believe that talent and 'natural ability' are more important, and that less effort is required. This leads you to avoid challenges, feel threatened by the success of others, avoid new experiences due to fear of failure, and ignore negative feedback even when it is relevant and useful. To have a fixed mindset causes you to want to protect your image, the idea that you are able or successful, rather than to actually risk failure by engaging with a challenge.

Growth mindset

Alternatively, with a growth mindset, you have the belief that your capacity for learning and intelligence can grow with time and experience. When you truly believe you can become smarter, you will realise that your effort affects your success, so you will be more willing to apply extra time and effort, leading to higher achievement. This mindset allows you to embrace challenges, to persevere in the face of failures and setbacks, find inspiration in the success of others, to accept criticism as a tool with which to improve, and most relevant to the current topic of discussion: a growth mindset helps you to look for people who challenge you to grow.

[For more detailed information on growth versus fixed mindset, read *Mindset* by Carol Dweck]

I have talked to you a lot about discipline, and I have skirted around the closely related topic of motivation. This is very important: you must understand motivation well; specifically how it is distinguished from discipline.

Motivation

If discipline is the quality of operating to a set of rules or standards you hold privately within yourself, then motivation can be understood as the utilisation of external factors as a force of influence. If you identify motivating forces in your own life and harness their impelling qualities, they may be used as a defence against laziness. Think carefully about what drives you to action, then carry these thoughts with you, always ready to use as a reminder of why you must act.

> *"The desire for rest is just weakness, it is only the desire to take the path of least resistance, the easy path. But by engaging in action one step at a time you will overcome that desire and you will stay on the disciplined path, the righteous path, the warpath, which is exactly where you belong."*
>
> **~ Jocko Willink**

Self-motivation does not exist.

> **The definition of motivation reads:**
>
> *A reason or reasons for acting or behaving in a particular way.*

If the reason for you to act or behave in a particular way is based on an internal set of rules, or a code of conduct you hold within yourself, that is *discipline*. If you are able to control yourself based on your own internal willpower, you are acting with discipline.

With this in mind, the only remaining cause of your motivation must be an external factor. If it is an external force, it cannot possibly be 'self' motivation. When you desire to either gain or avoid something outside of yourself, or are inspired by something you have seen or heard, you are being influenced by *motivation*.

Allow me to give you a military anecdote. During training, in the morning we would be woken by a corporal who would come into our bunk room yelling at us to haul our asses out of bed. What he was doing was motivating me to wake up. His words and actions were an external factor, motivating me to get out of bed. But what he was really trying to do was to instill discipline within me, so that eventually I would not need anyone yelling at me in the morning to get me out of bed, I would be able to get myself out of bed because I would have become a disciplined soldier. (This is an example of the corporal applying discipline as a verb)

Let me give you another example which may be a little more universal. Imagine, as a child, there's a jar of cookies in the kitchen, but your mother tells you that you may only have one per day. Well maybe at some point, when no one's around, you think you can take a couple more and get away with it. But of course your mother finds out, and she punishes you for it. Her punishment is motivation, so that in the future, when you see that jar of delicious cookies tempting you on the shelf, the thought of being punished, the fear of consequences motivates you to restrain yourself. This self-restraint develops discipline within you, so that in the future when you are tempted by anything, the metaphorical 'cookies' you often face in the world, you will have a more practiced and stronger degree of self-control with which to restrain yourself.

As we discussed previously on the topic of discipline, you can use strong and consistent motivation repeatedly over time to aid with the development of discipline within yourself.

Key points:

- ➢ Discipline is internal
- ➢ Motivation is external

You will encounter many people online who speak disparagingly of motivation, and encourage you to rely entirely on discipline. This is good advice, loosely speaking. However, very few people are fueled solely by unwavering discipline. A lot of people who claim to operate entirely on discipline are simply unaware of the motivating forces within their own lives.

Do not neglect motivation. Discipline is preferable: it is more consistent and reliable. But motivation is useful too; it has a valid place in your life, even if it's just listening to some of your favourite music when you're at the gym, or watching an inspirational YouTuber. These are effective and powerful tools.

One very important consideration that is worth being aware of, is that motivation is always the start of any endeavour. The absolute beginning of any activity is always spurred by motivation.

Right now, I do not play the violin. Why don't I play the violin? Is it because I have insufficient discipline? No. It is because I have never had the initial motivation to begin playing the violin in the first place.

There is always some initial motivating factor to the beginning of any pursuit you undertake, to condemn motivation entirely is to forget that fact.

In the book *Grit* by Angela Duckworth, she explains three stages of practice that are key to mastering a pursuit long-term: The first stage is to cultivate your interests, and simply enjoy what you are doing. The second is to develop a habit of daily challenge-exceeding-skill practice. The last is to connect your work to a purpose beyond yourself. People who are more experienced and claim to disregard motivation have simply forgotten what it was like to be a beginner; their advice should be taken with a grain of salt.

Identify motivating factors in your life: people you aspire to be like, your favorite books or movies that sparked your initial interest, your goals and the things you want to achieve. The key is that you must not cling to this motivation. The stronger you grasp onto motivation, the more you will suffer in its absence. Motivation is largely based on emotional links. As your emotions and feelings are transient in nature, they are not qualities you should rely on too heavily. Enjoy motivation while it's here, but don't spend too much time looking for it when it's gone.

> *"Motivation is a luxury, discipline is a necessity."*
>
> **~ Ian Abernethy**

First, you must become aware of our own laziness. Recognition leads to mindfulness. Once you are aware of laziness, you are able to consciously apply discipline.

Remember well, the four steps to developing internal discipline:

#1 - Strong Reason Why
#2 - Routine
#3 - If-Then Technique
#4 - Find a Teacher

Remain aware of external motivation, and utilise it effectively when it presents itself.

Once discipline is cultivated and you are mindful of motivation, the result is a state of flow in which effort finds you easily.

Restlessness

Restlessness has been described as the application of too much effort. However, I believe that we cannot apply too much effort, if it is implemented in the correct manner.

I prefer to think of restlessness as the *misapplication of effort*. Your mind is always working, always thinking, and when it wanders you can begin to feel agitated or distracted as you become lost in worry or filled with regret. Learning from past experiences is beneficial, but lingering feelings of remorse often have no merit and become psychologically damaging over time. Considering potential future events also has its advantages in preparation and planning, but again, you should be cautioned against losing yourself to anxiety and unproductive nervousness.

> *"Whatever an enemy might do to an enemy, or a foe to a foe, the ill-directed mind can do to you even worse."*
>
> **~ Udāna Pali Canon**

We all experience anxiety and depression at times, and to varying degrees of severity, these are normal feelings and part of the human condition. However, the rate at which people experience these feelings, and the strength with which they are consumed by them is increasing year by year. These hindrances, however grievous they may feel, are not emotions you are condemned to suffer hopelessly, nor are they immutable features of your personality that cannot be changed.

As with all hindrances: recognition leads to mindfulness. At the moment of realisation that your mind has been lost in restless thought you consciously separate yourself from the experience.

Practice this well, and through repetition you will extend the gap between yourself and your feelings.

If projecting your thoughts into the future leads to anxiety, and reminiscing over memories of the past leads to depression, where else are you left to go?

Here and Now

This present moment, right now, as you read these words.

Albert Einstein famously said "Time is an illusion", a fabricated concept, but he wasn't the first to say this. The *Eternal Now* is a perennial quality that has been spoken of in all religions and philosophical texts throughout recorded history.

> *"We are here and it is now. Further than that all human knowledge is moonshine."*
>
> **~ H.L. Mencken**

People often think of time as a reel of film, stretching infinitely into the future and disappearing far off into the past, with the present moment a single fraction of time caught in the middle. But the past is a memory of a present moment that no longer exists, and the future is a purely imagined scenario projected forward, based upon your previous experience.

> *"What you perceive as future is an intrinsic part of your state of consciousness now. If your mind carries a heavy burden of past, you will experience more of the same. The past perpetuates itself through lack of presence. The quality of your consciousness at this moment is what shapes the future - which, of course, can only be experienced as the Now."*
>
> **~ Eckhart Tolle**

When you understand fully that neither the past nor the future exist in any tangible way, you will realise all that is left is this present moment. The present moment is unbounded. It stretches infinitely in all directions, rather than being a thin wafer stuck between two endless expanses of 'before' and 'after'. There is only Now: a ceaselessly changing event with no beginning and no end.

> *"There is surely nothing other than the single purpose of the present moment. A man's whole life is a succession of moment after moment. If one fully understands the present moment, there will be nothing else to do, and nothing else to pursue. Live being true to the single purpose of the moment."*
>
> **~ Yamamoto Tsunetomo**

All this metaphysical philosophy is really neat, but it doesn't help to free yourself from worrying about what Brian said in the office last Friday, or the tax return that's due next week.

How do you consciously bring yourself into this present moment, right now?

Meditation

Extensive research involving the world's top neuroscientists and most cutting-edge technology confirms many of the benefits of meditation, which has been practised and taught formally for thousands of years. Enhanced concentration and focus, improved memory and sleep, increased self-awareness and tolerance to pain, reduced symptoms of stress, anxiety and depression, as well as measurable improvements to physical health - these are just some of the many benefits of meditation that have been proven by peer-reviewed clinical studies.

The true value of meditation is immeasurable, and cannot be conveyed by words. It can only be experienced by you, the individual. The measurable qualities which can be studied and recorded represent only the surface of what can be achieved. The many ways in which meditation will change your life and revolutionise your entire perspective of reality are so profound and momentous that they completely transcend the narrow limitations of spoken and written language.

> *"All of humanity's problems stem from man's inability to sit quietly in a room alone."*
>
> **~ Blaise Pascal**

The practice of meditation is vast and deep. There is a lot to learn, and for most people even an entire lifetime of dedicated practise would not uncover all there is to experience. But don't worry: the good news is that the barrier to entry is extremely low, it's super easy to start, right now! (What other time could you possibly start, than Now?)

Posture and Breathing

First, sit up straight. Rule #3: Posture

The techniques and practices employed within meditation are to be used at all times. Truly, when there is no longer distinction between 'meditation' and regular life, you have reached an enlightened state of being. Until you have reached that point, however, you must practise formal seated meditation.

Seated meditation can be practised on a chair, but it is best if you sit on the floor, on a firm cushion with your hips raised 3-4 inches from the floor. Have a look online at zafu meditation cushions when you are ready to invest in your practice. Having your hips raised is vital to sitting comfortably for long periods: it is much easier to sit with a level pelvis and a straight back when your hips are higher than your knees.

My personal preference is the half-lotus position, but you can sit in the full lotus if you prefer, or if your legs are less mobile I recommend the Burmese position, as pictured below.

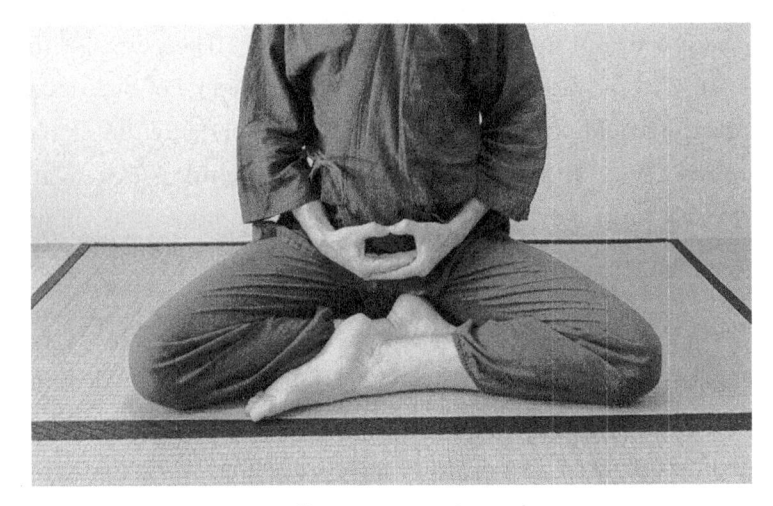

Burmese position

Half lotus position

Full lotus position

The most important thing is that your knees are on the floor. You must have three points of contact between your bum, and both knees. Lean forward as you are sitting down, place all your weight onto your knees and then sit back onto the cushion. If there is a gap between your knees and the ground, place a small cushion beneath the raised knee until you become more comfortable in the position and are able to sit without it.

The effort applied to sit in such a way is well spent. I guarantee that no matter how uncomfortable or unusual this position may initially feel, after just a few weeks of consistent practice your body will adapt to this natural position, and you will eventually be able to sit almost indefinitely.

If you experience any pain or major issues, please consult a doctor, physical therapist or yoga instructor for further assistance.

Once you are comfortable and sitting upright, bring the focus of your attention to your breath. *Rule #1: Breathe*

Don't worry about trying to change anything. We began this book with a brief instruction on how to deepen and lengthen your breath; if you are able to comfortably do that, please do so now. If not, don't worry about it, just bring your attention to the breath.

We are not judging the breath: it does not matter so much if it is short and shallow, or long and deep. All I want you to do is watch the breath. Feel the flow of air through your nose. Be aware of any movement in your stomach, chest or shoulders. Concentrate on the breath. Examine it as though you are watching the breath of another person, as if you are following the breath of someone sitting beside you. There is no hurry: just sit and watch.

Posture and breathing.

When you become distracted and begin to wander in thought, that is fine; don't beat yourself up about it. Just bring yourself back to the posture, and back to the breathing.

I said 'when' you become distracted, not 'if'. Because this is a matter of absolute certainty. Do not feel frustrated or disappointed when you realise that your concentration has broken: the natural state of the mind is to think and consider, to ruminate and ponder. The key you are looking for is that brief moment of clarity. When you become aware that you have been distracted, rejoice! In that exact moment you are no longer distracted. Recognition leads to mindfulness.

It will also help your practice to count your breaths. On your first exhale, count '1'. And then '2' on the next outward breath, and then '3' after that... All the way up to '10'. Once you reach '10' or become distracted (whichever comes first), return to '1' on the next exhalation.

Think of this practice like lifting weights. Each time your mind wanders (whether it takes a few seconds or a few minutes), eventually you will become aware that you are no longer concentrating on the breath. Once you recognise this distraction, without judgement or frustration, simply bring yourself back to the posture, and then back to the breathing. This is one rep. Each time you repeat this process, of concentration - distraction - realisation - concentration, you are performing repetitions of the exercise. As you perform more repetitions and continue your practice, your concentration will strengthen, you will be able to hold your focus for longer, and realise more quickly when your mind has begun to wander.

> *"This is why all the great Asian philosophies begin with the practice of concentration, that is, of attentive looking. It is as if to say, "If you want to know what reality is, you must look directly at it and see for yourself. But this needs a certain kind of concentration, because reality is not symbols, it is not words and thoughts, it is not reflections and fantasies. Therefore to see it clearly, your mind must be free from wandering words and from the floating fantasies of memory."*
>
> **~ Alan Watts**

In the same way that you are always in some posture or another, you are also always breathing. These are your two base qualities: posture and breathing. Two fundamental activities you cannot remove yourself from. You can add to these, with cooking, cleaning, reading, sleeping, talking, anything at all. But you cannot reduce yourself to any less than these two activities: Posture and breathing.

> *"The objective of meditation is not to quiet the mind. The objective of meditation is to know whatever is happening as it is. If the mind is quiet, then it's quiet. If it's not quiet, it's not quiet. Just know that."*
>
> **~ Sayadaw U Tejanija**

By focusing on your posture and your breathing, for as long as you are able to hold your concentration, you are *here and now*.

Two key features of your posture and your breath are that they are always here and now. Your posture cannot be anywhere but here, and your breathing cannot exist at any time other than now. To pay proper attention to your posture and breathing you must necessarily let go of time, abandon all thought of past and future, and give yourself entirely to this present moment.
In this way, meditation can also be used as an antidote for desire, anger, and many other internal challenges you face.

The practice of meditation requires time and effort to cultivate, and it is difficult to measure progress, but I implore you to consider this practice mandatory.

> *"...there is no need to blindly believe anything, the true deep understanding will come from your own experience in meditation."*
>
> **~ Joseph Goldstein**

There is no other practice so universally accessible, with such unbelievable benefits and so desperately required by modern society, as meditation. As I previously said, the practice of meditation is vast and deep, and there is much to learn, but with the techniques you have learnt already you are able to begin your practice today. Sit for just ten minutes, with no expectation of anything, and with no judgement of your own performance. Only sit. Correct your posture, draw your attention to the breath, and once you realise you have been distracted, start again.

> *"Intuition, wisdom, physical action, are always one. That is the secret of meditation, and of the martial arts."*
>
> **~ Taisen Deshimaru**

Posture and breathing. Here and Now.

Present Awareness

> *"To understand reality as a direct experience is the reason we practice meditation, and the reason we study Buddhism."*
>
> **~ Shunryu Suzuki**

We are able to describe the theoretical understanding and practical application of meditation with the single, unifying principle of 'Present Awareness'. Present, in both time and space, with the knowledge that the only true time is now, and the only location you will ever exist is here. Awareness, as the practice of meditation is that of cultivating clear, penetrating awareness of your current experience. This phrase encompasses both the realisation of the Eternal Now, and also the empirical practice of meditation itself. As you study and as you sit, you cultivate Present Awareness. Keep this expression in the forefront of your mind as a guiding principle to your practice.

Correct effort

We have spoken of laziness, and we have talked about restlessness, now is the perfect time to discuss the correct balance of effort. This is the first and most common hurdle all my students face when they begin any new practice; whether it is in meditation, martial arts, exercise, diet, study, or anything else.

> *"No one succeeds without effort. Mind control is not your birthright. Those who succeed owe their success to their perseverance."*
>
> **~ Ramana Maharshi**

Before you begin a new practice you apply no effort: you only have thoughts and aspirations toward your goals. Once you start, especially if you are high in motivation, you may apply great effort, which is fantastic but often unsustainable. This is a marathon, not a sprint. If you go full force from the word 'Go', you are almost guaranteed to overwhelm yourself and break your rhythm. And what happens when you stumble in your practice? That is exactly where a lot of people give up.

"I failed."
"I can't do it, it's too hard."
"How can I possibly keep this up for a year, or more? It's impossible."
Sound familiar?

I see it time and time again. I know exactly how you feel. You want to see results, you set high expectations for yourself and compare your progress to the most successful people in your field. This is too much pressure. Setting lofty goals and striving for the best is fantastic: I completely support that mindset. But if you apply such great pressure to yourself and force too much effort too early, your spirit can break, and that's when we see people give up entirely.

> *"Milarepa, the famous Tibetan yogi, advised his disciples to 'hasten slowly.' Hasten in the sense of being continuous and unrelenting in your effort, but do so with poise and equanimity. Persistent and full of effort, yet very relaxed and balanced."*
>
> **~ Joseph Goldstein**

You cannot apply 'too much effort', if it is applied conscientiously and without stress. But rare is the individual with such mindfulness and presence.

Balance is key. The Middle Way.

The balance required is unique within each of us, with our own personal qualities and attributes, we each have a different tolerance for various stressors in life. You must be your own judge. This requires sharp introspection and keen self-awareness. Assess yourself critically: where are you applying too little effort? Be honest about where you need to push yourself and increase the tempo. And so too, be mindful of when you are applying too great an effort. Know when to slow it down, to be patient, to consolidate your gains and recharge your energy.

Apply this balance of effort on both the micro and macro scale of life. On the micro scale, our energy levels, concentration and motivation fluctuate on an hourly basis. Throughout the day, be aware of when you need to kick your ass off the sofa, drink some coffee and get to work, and when you need to sit down, take a deep breath, meditate or read a book. On the macro scale, assess your overall personality, consider your character traits, speak with trusted friends and family if you need a more objective opinion. If you know that you are prone to laziness, focus on building discipline and harnessing motivation. Or if you think you're wound a little too tight and need to ease off the gas: meditate more. Be aware of the stress and pressure you exert on yourself and apply the remedy of present awareness.

> *"Effort within the mind further limits the mind, because effort implies struggle towards a goal and when you have a goal, a purpose, an end in view, you have placed a limit on the mind."*
>
> **~ Bruce Lee**

Do not forget that *balance is key*, you must apply *the Middle Way* in all things.

Doubt

The uncertainty and lack of conviction within doubt will single-handedly kill your progress dead in its tracks. The crippling nature of doubt is often experienced as a lack of confidence in either your abilities or your knowledge, leading you toward low morale, reluctance and trepidation. This psychological barrier will then lead to physical obstacles, as doubt redirects your actions and causes you to seek the easy option, the path of least resistance, the downhill road. Much like anger, it is very easy to feel a sense of justification within doubt. It can disguise itself as critical thinking and fool you into rationalising any evasive or uncertain action you take.

Feelings of doubt can be compounded by other hindrances, such as aversion toward effort, or feelings of worry, or annoyance that you may not be progressing as you think you should. Some people reminisce about times when they were filled with motivation and determination, convincing themselves that they cannot continue without feeling such emotions once more.

Confidence is critical to success. You begin any mission with the firm belief that it is possible to accomplish your tasks. When you inevitably encounter resistance, when you experience setbacks and small failures, doubt can begin to creep in and increase the difficulty.

> *"During times of peace when listening to stories of battle, one should never say, "In facing such a situation, what would a person do?" Such words are out of the question. How will a man who has doubts even in his own room achieve anything on the*

> *battlefield? There is a saying that goes, "No matter what the circumstances might be, one should be of the mind to win. One should be holding the first spear to strike."*
>
> **~Yamamoto Tsunetomo,
> quoting Lord Naoshige in the Hagakure**

It is possible to dispel doubt. I am going to arm you with the weapons you need to conquer your own apprehension: two clear techniques that even the most timid novice can use to strike forth with confidence.

To begin, you know what's coming: Recognition leads to mindfulness.
Like a diligent soldier on standing guard, you must remain alert and aware of the shadowy, insipid nature of doubt. Are these feelings of apprehension and uncertainty well founded? A gut feeling trying to warn you of danger? Or is doubt playing its tricks on you; the devil whispering in your ear, convincing you to sabotage your own work?

Faith

The antidote to doubt is faith.

Not blind faith. Not questionless submission, as is often prescribed like a sedative to numb the pain of life. Blind faith is irrational faith, and irrational faith leads to irrational behaviour. I am not asking you to "fake it 'till you make it", which sometimes works, but when you build a house without foundations, it will collapse when tested.

Faith in yourself, and your past experience

Believe in yourself.

I know it sounds trite and played out, but listen to what I'm telling you here. You are not a fool. You would not have undertaken this task if it was not possible to achieve, if you weren't interested, and if you didn't think it would benefit you. You knew it was going to be difficult: the best things always are. Well here you are, in that moment of difficulty. Don't give up now, stay true to the decision you made to pursue this goal. Have faith in the choice you made to undertake this task.

Have faith in your past experience. This ain't your first rodeo, you've challenged yourself before, and whatever the outcome I am sure you learnt from it. Small victories build self-confidence. Call to mind your past successes; the times you overcame yourself and accomplished what you previously thought impossible.

US Navy SEAL and ultra-marathon runner David Goggins calls this 'reaching into the cookie jar'. Write a list of your greatest feats of accomplishment. When you hit the wall and begin to question yourself, reach into your memory, remember what you have achieved in the past, and call to mind the victories and successes that made you who you are today.

I remember when I went to my first muay thai gym, walking in as a less than a novice, with zero experience and rock-bottom physicality. My gym usually split the class into three groups, beginners, advanced, and those training for fights. When I first joined the gym I was way back near the entrance, the closest to the door and bottom of the pecking order. I remember looking up at the guys sparring in the ring, dreaming all kinds of dreams. Then a few years later, I wasn't just training in the ring, I was teaching the classes.

Even if the task you're currently undertaking is a whole new field you have no experience in, have faith in your ability to learn. I was a terrible student in school. When I was very young I found school easy and was ahead of most other students, this gave me a chip on my shoulder which led to a fixed mindset, and ended up crippling the rest of my academic life. I never studied and left school with no qualifications.
However, since then I have pursued many new subjects, several of them to the point at which I teach them professionally. This has taken a great deal of time and effort, but it has given me faith in my own ability to learn.

> *"There was a time when I met luck at every turn.' But luck is the good fortune you determine for yourself: and good fortune consists in good inclinations of the soul, good impulses, good action."*
>
> **~ Marcus Aurelius**

Have confidence: as long as you apply yourself correctly in any new task you undertake, you can have absolute faith that there is nothing you cannot learn.

Faith in the process, and your teachers

Success is never an accident, but the progressive realisation of a worthy goal.

For you to achieve the tasks you have laid out for yourself, you must have a plan. If you do not have a clearly structured system to guide yourself toward your aims, you are like a ship, cast off with a torn sail and a broken rudder, your destination entrusted to the whims of fate.

Examine the processes which have worked for other people. Search for individuals or groups who are currently in the position you wish to be, and find out what they did to get there. Do not be afraid to ask them directly: successful people are often the most helpful people you will ever meet.

You do not need to be able to understand the process perfectly for it to work. If you already understood exactly how to reach your goals you wouldn't need any help in the first place. Have faith in the process, and confidence that you are a capable individual. If it has worked for others, it can work for you.

As you look at the processes involved in reaching your goals, stay vigilant and on the lookout for worthy teachers. We spoke about this previously on the fourth step to building discipline: *Find a Teacher*.

A good teacher will have already encountered and overcome the mistakes you are bound to make, both for themselves, and whilst helping other people too, people just like you. Having faith in your teacher and applying their advice will fast-track your progress and shave years off the process.

The greatest benefit of all in having a teacher, is that they will be able to correct mistakes that you aren't even aware you are making. This has become most apparent to me in practising and teaching Martial Arts. Without having an experienced observer, you can continue to make mistakes that will compound over time and may never be corrected, this is especially true for beginners.

> *"To one who has faith, no explanation is necessary. To one without faith, no explanation is possible."*
>
> **~ Thomas Aquinas**

Doubt is a challenging hindrance to deal with, and it often affects intelligent people the most, as a highly intellectual person is capable of forming a strong argument, and talking themselves out of action.

You must accept that you do not have all the answers, and there are many things you have no experience in. At this time you can rely on faith. Faith in yourself and your past experience, as well as faith in the process and your teachers.

> *"It is a principle of the art of war that one should simply lay down his life and strike. If one's opponent also does the same, it is an even match. Defeating one's opponent is then a matter of faith and destiny."*
>
> **~ Yamamoto Tsunetomo**

The Five Hindrances:

- Desire
- Anger
- Laziness
- Restlessness
- Doubt

Your primary defence against these hardships is recognition. Recognition leads to mindfulness. However, beyond mindfulness we are able to apply certain remedies to counteract and transcend these difficulties.

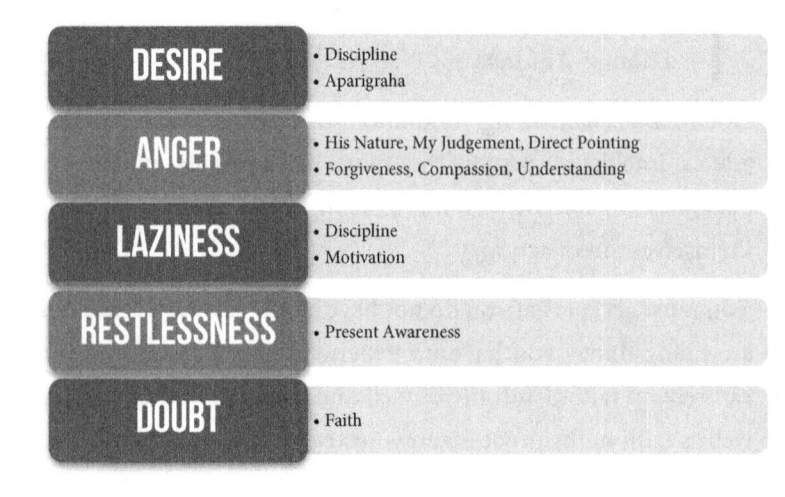

Hindrance	Remedies
DESIRE	• Discipline • Aparigraha
ANGER	• His Nature, My Judgement, Direct Pointing • Forgiveness, Compassion, Understanding
LAZINESS	• Discipline • Motivation
RESTLESSNESS	• Present Awareness
DOUBT	• Faith

Take your time implementing these systems. It will take months or even years of determined practise and consideration before they become an intrinsic part of your normal mindset. But when they do, full realisation of the Five Hindrances and their curative virtues will transform your life.

Diligent application of effort is required to learn these methods and ingrain them into your mode of being. To keep the systems and principles you have learnt foremost in your mind, there is one simple practice which predates recorded history, and will assist you in embedding any knowledge deep into your subconscious.

CHAPTER 4
DAILY MANTRA

By the mercy of my teachers and the benefit of years of study, practise, trial and error, I have developed the systems I share with you now. But it is not good enough to simply be told something once. No one has the perfect retention of information to remember absolutely everything the first time they are taught it. Especially when required to recall that knowledge under pressure.

> *"Something that can never be learnt too thoroughly can never be said too often. With some people you only need to point to a remedy; others need to have it rammed into them."*
>
> **~ Seneca**

It's a lot easier to remember the things you have been taught whilst you're sitting at home, nice and comfortable in a warm and quiet environment. But when you're out in the world, in unfamiliar territory, dealing with hostile forces, with no time to think or consider carefully how to react, that's when you are only able to respond using the tools you have retained with repetition and practice.

To remember and reinforce some of the most important lessons I have learnt in my adult life, I have developed a daily mantra. I recite this mantra several times a day without exception: as part of my morning routine, at the beginning of meditation, and in bed before going to sleep. I also repeat the mantra during other moments of opportunity, such as whilst walking somewhere, or sitting in a train or waiting room. This consistent, daily repetition is a powerful force, working to engrave the most important and valuable lessons I have learnt into my mind, so that I never forget them, and I am able to recall them without hesitation.

The recitation of mantras has been used in the transmission and preservation of teachings for thousands of years, since long before recorded history. In Hinduism, Buddhism and Taoism, spoken sutras were originally used to convey ancient lessons and teachings across entire continents, in a time long before mass print, in which most people could not read or write.

Repetition of a mantra has the same benefits as spoken affirmations, it will focus your goals and intentions, reprogram

THE MARTIAL METHOD

negative thought patterns into positive ones, increase confidence and motivate you into taking action. You must program yourself, or allow yourself to be programmed by others. By creating a mantra you clearly define your base operating system, and remind yourself daily of the core tenets and principles by which you choose to live.

First I will share with you my personal mantra, then I will explain to you how to develop your own.

My mantra began many years ago with a single line: "All is as thinking makes it so." The most critical, and powerful passage from Marcus Aurelius' Meditations.

This one sentence I would recite on an exhalation, either verbally, or silently within my mind. In exactly the same way that we count our breaths during meditation; I take a nice comfortable breath in, then as I breathe out I repeat the passage, "All is as thinking makes it so."

This is the method I employ for reciting each line of my entire mantra, which is currently 60 lines long and takes approximately seven minutes to deliver entirely.

As of May 2021, my daily mantra is as follows:

> Su-u, haku
>
> Ichi
> Ni
> San
> Yon

LEWIS E. BRIGGS

> Go
> Roku
> Nana
> Hachi
> Kyuu
> Juu
>
> All is as thinking makes it so
>
> Recognition leads to mindfulness
>
> Knowledgeable and Wise
> Physically Skilled and Able
> Disciplined and Diligent
> Stoic and Composed
> Resolute and Without Regret
> Fearless and Courageous
> Ferocious and Without Mercy
> Honourable and With Zen
>
> 30170125
>
> I do my own duty,
> The other things do not distract me
>
> Matters of great concern should be treated lightly,
> Matters of small concern should be treated seriously
>
> The Sage never attempts great things
> And thus accomplishes them

THE MARTIAL METHOD

No action should be undertaken without aim,
Or other than in conformity with a principle
Affirming the art of life

No rest is worth anything,
Except that which is earned

You have a right to your actions, but never your actions' fruit
Indifferent to gain or loss, to victory or defeat
Act for action's sake, with no concern for results

His nature, my judgement, direct pointing

Today is victory over myself of yesterday;
Tomorrow is my victory over lesser men

Do not criticise, condemn or complain
Give honest and sincere appreciation
Arouse in the other person an eager want

Venerate Gods and Buddhas, but do not rely on them
Abandon self interest, do not seek fame or fortune
Always remain true to the Way of a Warrior

Concentration, clarity and equanimity
Sight, sound and body sensation
Mental image, talk, and body emotion
Impermanent, unsatisfactory and no-self

The Buddha, Dharma, Sangha

> The perfect man employs his mind as a mirror
> It grasps nothing; it refuses nothing
> It receives, but does not keep
>
> Those on the Way, become the Way
>
> Maintain Zen - present awareness
>
> Here and Now
>
> Tao k'o Tao fei ch'ang Tao
>
> .
> .
> .

***

As well as my own maxims, this mantra contains quotes and passages from Marcus Aurelius, Lao Tzu, Yamamoto Tsunetomo, Miyamoto Musashi, Dale Carnegie, Shinzen Young and the Bhagavad Gita, among others.

What I don't want you to do is simply copy my mantra. These are lessons and principles that are important to me. I want you to think about the standards and virtues that are important to you.

It doesn't need to be anywhere near as long as my mantra. I know mine has become quite lengthy indeed! But all of the passages included within are important to me, and I cannot currently bring myself to omit any of them. Remember that I began my mantra with a single passage, 'All is as thinking makes it so.' Start simple, fundamental, and build from there.

Think about what is important to you. Think about the teachers and sources of information most influential in your life.

If you are struggling to think of anything significant to begin with, that's alright; don't force anything. Search out those teachers, read more, join the right groups. If nothing else, you have already begun your journey with the purchase of this book, and can use the lessons you have learnt already: The Three Rules, The Five Hindrances. When you encounter compelling lessons from the teachers and literature in your life, do not rely only on your memory to preserve them. If it is something that resonates with you, write it down, study it, keep a record of the things you learn. From there, when you find the axioms by which you intend to live your life, then you are ready to develop your own mantra.

Once you have the beginnings of your own personal mantra, you must make a habit of regular recitation. Include the practice into your daily routine, and also into short times in which you find yourself free; on the bus, walking to work, waiting for the kettle to boil, times in which your natural habit may be to look at your phone. This too is a form of meditation. Like a computer rebooting its systems, by focusing your attention, clearing your thoughts, and reminding yourself of the core rules and tenets by which you intend to live, you will have consciously reset yourself, in this present moment, and be ready to engage the world.

CHAPTER 5
SIXTEEN VIRTUES OF ACHILLEUS

Creating your own deity

> *"Aristotle defined the virtues simply as the ways of behaving that are most conducive to happiness in life. Vice was defined as the ways of behaving least conducive to happiness. He observed that the virtues always aim for balance and avoid the extremes of the vices. Cultivating judgement about the difference between virtue and vice is the beginning of wisdom."*
>
> ~ **Dr Norman Doidge**

Ask any of the kids around you today who their heroes are. Captain America, Princess Elsa or Han Solo are likely candidates, Disney has an increasing monopoly on our children's role models. Thousands of years ago you may have been told Zeus, Hercules, or Beowulf.

Who are your role models? What characters, either real or fictional, serve as your inspiration and paragons of virtue? Think carefully of the examples by which you attempt to live your life. But more than this, consider specifically, what is it about their nature that is so virtuous?

Throughout history we have had a pantheon of gods and mythical heroes to inspire us and serve as the personification of our most venerable merits and attributes. However, as Nietzsche famously proclaimed "God is dead. God remains dead. And we have killed him." And so we discarded our heavenly archetypes, developed over countless generations of tradition and heritage, and replaced them with what? Superheroes and cartoon characters, ill-conceived figures, designed for profit.

After many years of training, study and practice, I have asked myself clearly, what are the virtues by which I must live? Who is the God I serve, and what qualities does he embody? I set about creating my own avatar to which I direct my ambitions. After deep reflection and careful consideration I came to venerate these: the Sixteen Virtues of the Martial Deity.

Knowledgeable	Wise	Physically Skilled	Able
Disciplined	Diligent	Stoic	Composed
Resolute	Without Regret	Fearless	Courageous
Ferocious	Without Mercy	Honourable	With Zen

These are the Sixteen virtues by which I define my personal Deity. They cover physical, intellectual and spiritual qualities, as well as traditional masculine traits, and a careful balance between strength and benevolence. They are inspired from the plethora of real world teachers I have had the fortune to learn from, from my experience working in the military, private security, martial arts, and as a personal trainer, as well as the great patriarchs of antiquity I have learnt from through their surviving texts.

As with the daily mantra, you should start small and fundamental, take your time, and think carefully of the qualities you deem important. If you have not yet had the opportunity to learn from many inspirational teachers, don't worry about it. Keep reading, maintain your search, and stay open to new possibilities. As you continue to challenge yourself and walk the path of self-improvement you will meet admirable people with valuable lessons to share. No one is perfect, everyone has their faults. But for each of the successful, inspirational people you encounter, you can identify the traits that set them apart, and from these you are able to create an amalgamation, a composite character representing your North star, your ideal to strive toward.

As you list the characteristics of your own icon, the character will begin to take a more defined shape in your mind, becoming increasingly vivid. Once you have determined the qualities of your deity, you must name him. Nothing in life exists clearly without a name to distinguish it from the rest.

I name my Martial Deity; Achilleus.
But of course, the mighty Achilleus! Son of Peleus, the greatest of all Greek warriors and hero of the Trojan War. As recounted in Homer's Iliad, which alone is one of the greatest works of European literature and a cornerstone of Western civilisation.

You may remember these virtues as being listed in my daily mantra. The Sixteen Virtues of Achilleus became a foundational part of my mantra, and I advise you to do the same. I will not explain the attributes I have chosen in detail. The reasons I have selected them specifically, and the origins of their value are distinctly relevant to me. You are to develop your own daily mantra, and so too must you consider the virtues of your own Deity, be it one, or many.

> *"Mentorship needn't be total duplication. I'm not trying to become my mentors, I'm using them as a focal point to help me summon and nurture latent qualities which, without stewardship, I may not be able to realise."*
>
> **~ Russell Brand**

Today's homework:
Get a pen and paper, sit down, and write out the virtues you hold in high regard. Take your time, you don't have to finish this exercise in one sitting. In fact, it's better if you spend a few days reflecting on it deeply. Think of both fictional and real world examples, try to cover every important facet of being, see if you can pare down similar characteristics into a single quality.

Once you have whittled it down to those key virtues of utmost importance, write it down neatly and stick it up somewhere you will see it every day. Read it aloud first thing in the morning and last thing at night. Revise it constantly until you are able to recite it without difficulty from memory.

Name your Deity.
You can even go so far as to give them a back-story. What does your character look like? If you have any artistic talent, feel free to draw a picture. All of these tasks go a long way to clarifying the image in your mind, to take it from being vague and idealistic, to making it certain and concrete. The clearer you are

able to make your archetype in your mind, the more accurately you will be able to pursue this paragon.

Think how many statues have been erected in honour of our greatest deities, how many temples constructed, paintings painted, songs written, stories told; all to uphold an ideal, to preserve virtues worth striving for. For as long as human civilization has existed, we have exalted heroes, and venerated the ideals that have defined them. So many of these temples, great monuments and holy relics are now laid to waste, or if preserved, have been relegated to museum trinkets and historical novelties, their sacred value long forgotten.

If Nietzsche was right and God is in fact dead, he can be reborn again.

First, distinctly conceive the figure and characteristics of your Deity. Second, carefully recite and memorise the virtues for which he or she stands. Last, ask yourself frequently, as you live and pursue your daily life:

> *"Are my actions in accordance with the virtues of the Martial Deity?"*

CHAPTER 6
MEMENTO MORI

Memento is the Latin 2nd person singular active imperative of *meminī* 'to remember, to bear in mind', usually serving as a warning: "remember!" Mori is the present infinitive of the deponent verb *morior* 'to die'.

Memento Mori: "Remember you will die."

From the first moment you draw breath, you are eligible to die. Most people don't like to consider their own mortality, even though it is the only universal experience guaranteed to every living creature. Every day people die in the prime of their lives, often at peak physical condition, but we don't want to consider that it could happen to us.

> *"How strange that this sole thing that is certain and common to all, exercises almost no influence on men, and that they are the furthest from regarding themselves as the brotherhood of death!"*
>
> **~ Friedrich Nietzsche, The Gay Science**

You may consider that thinking about death is morbid and depressing, and we should focus on life and positivity. Countless philosophers, theologians and psychologists have discussed the reality of death throughout recorded history, and have concluded that thinking about death is in fact life enhancing.

> *"Virtually every great thinker has thought deeply and written about death; and many have concluded that death is inextricably a part of life, and that lifelong consideration of death enriches rather than impoverishes life."*
>
> **~ Irvin Yalom, Existential Psychotherapy**

Consider how dramatically a person's behaviour can change when they have a near-death experience. Meanwhile, psychiatrists and clinical psychologists often struggle desperately to induce even slight positive changes to a person's character. If a person is convinced they are about to die before being granted the gift of more life, very often that individual will exhibit a dramatic psychological transformation.

Of course, it is not recommended to intentionally risk death merely to improve our psychological health. You can however experience similar, albeit less dramatic effects by periodically contemplating death.

> *"Though the physicality of death destroys an individual, the idea of death can save him."*
> **~ Irvin Yalom**

Reflecting on the brief and tenuous nature of existence can aid you for one simple reason: it provides you with an accurate and realistic perspective of life.

To live fully you must be aware of your limitations, the most significant of which is the scarcity and uncertain duration of time you have been granted. Failure to recognise this limitation and live accordingly is one of the most tragic habits of mankind, as it often leads people to sacrifice and depreciate the present in the false hope that there will always be a future in which to make up for it.

> *"You may leave this life at any moment: have this possibility in your mind in all that you do or say or think."*
> **~ Marcus Aurelius, Meditations**

Far too many people waste a great amount of time on pursuits which contribute little of positive value to their lives. Working dead-end jobs they hate, in unhealthy relationships with people they'd be better off without, unable or unwilling to escape destructive habits, and so much more besides. Along with giving you a greater appreciation of the present moment, contemplating death also helps you grasp the truth in Henry David Thoreau's statement, "The price of anything is the amount of life you exchange for it." People often understand that they need to change, to stop wasting time and to focus their efforts elsewhere. But they delay action, and justify putting it off with the excuse that conditions will be more ideal in the future.

> *"Just where death is expecting us is something we cannot know; so, for our part, expect him everywhere."*
>
> **~ Seneca**

As you consider the true nature of mortality and become more acutely aware of the finite amount of time you have remaining, recognition of your own impending death will imbue your life with a new sense of urgency, and help you to understand that with this inevitable conclusion approaching... "Existence cannot be postponed." (Irvin Yalom) Waiting for ideal future conditions is a risky gamble to make.

> *"Meditation on inevitable death should be performed daily. Every day when one's body and mind are at peace, one should meditate upon being ripped apart by arrows, rifles, spears and swords, being carried away by surging waves, being thrown into the midst of a great fire, being struck by lightning, being shaken to death by a great earthquake, falling from thousand-*

> *foot cliffs, dying of disease, or committing seppuku at the death of one's master. And every day without fail one should consider himself as dead. There is a saying of the elders that goes, "Step from under the eaves and you're a dead man. Leave the gate and the enemy is waiting." This is not a matter of being careful. It is to consider oneself as dead beforehand."*
>
> **~ Yamamoto Tsunetomo, Hagakure**

Periodically contemplating death can also improve your relationships with others. If you are more aware of your own mortality, you will also become more aware that the lives of everyone you care about are just as precariously hanging by a thread. Never knowing when it will be the final time in which you see someone will make you more appreciative of the limited time you are able to spend with them.

> *"Students of the Way, it goes without saying that you must consider the inevitability of death. Even if you don't consider this right now, you should be resolved not to waste time and refrain from doing meaningless things. You should spend your time carrying out what is worth doing. Among the things you should do, what is the most important? You must understand that all deeds other than those of the Buddhas and patriarchs are useless."*
>
> **~ Dōgen Zenji, Shōbōgenzō Zuimonki**

The benefits of contemplating death are undeniable, and yet most people avoid this practice with the attitude that we are better off rejecting such thoughts. Here too we must find balance. Death is an integral part of life, but to focus on it for too long will lead to paralysing anxiety and crippling dread. But to turn away from it completely is just as bad. Periodically contemplating death is necessary to imbue life with a much needed sense of urgency, and a sharp appreciation for the present moment that most people are entirely devoid of.

> *"No you do not have thousands of years to live. Urgency is on you. While you live, while you can, become good."*
>
> **~ Marcus Aurelius**

CHAPTER 7
ACTION

> *"Only those under Heaven who are absolutely sincere can develop their nature to the fullest."*
>
> **~ Chung-ni**

This entire book is worthless, everything I have shared with you is utterly meaningless, if you do not apply it.

> *"How does your directing mind employ itself? This is the whole issue. All else, of your own choice or not, is just corpse and smoke."*
>
> **~ Marcus Aurelius**

I know your life is not without fault, that you face difficulties and wish to transcend yourself. You are not alone, there are many alongside you who walk the path. What I offer you here is nothing new. This is ancient knowledge, which has been practised and shared for thousands of years in every continent of the world. I am sure you understand everything I have written in this book. I do not believe any of the rules or lessons to be especially challenging to grasp. But I assure you: there is a vast gulf between understanding the lessons theoretically and practically applying them to your life.

You must realise and truly understand the immeasurable difference between intellectual and experiential knowledge. It is a common pitfall for highly intelligent people to believe that understanding an idea conceptually is the same as experiencing it.

Frank Jackson proposed in his article "Epiphenomenal Qualia" a knowledge argument popularly known as 'Mary's Room'. In this philosophical thought experiment, Jackson tells the story of a scientist trapped in a black and white room, who can experience the world only through a black and white TV. The question is; if Mary is given all possible information about colour, how light interacts with the retina, how the brain perceives certain wavelengths, and so on... Does she then experience anything new when she steps out of the room and actually sees colour for the first time?

Let me ask you this: as a child, as much as your parents told you to be careful around fire, how dangerous it is, how it will hurt if you touch it, did you not learn a valuable and penetrating lesson the first time you got burnt?
A small taste of satori!

> *"A child certainly allows himself to be impressed by the grand talk of his parents, but do they really imagine he is educated by it? Actually it is the parents' lives that educate the child - what they add by word at best only serves to confuse him."*
>
> **~ Carl Jung**

Every waking moment is a test, and an opportunity to apply what you have learnt. Whether you make your bed in the morning, take the stairs instead of the escalator, pick up a book and study when you could watch Netflix, smile when someone cuts you off in traffic or hold yourself accountable when someone else is clearly to blame. The depth of our realisation of the Way is reflected in the smallest of actions.

> *" 'Marvelous Function'*
> *For a realisation to be authentic, one must be able to apply it in the actual world. True understanding is reflected in one's technique and also in one's daily life. This is the real battlefield where one's enlightenment is constantly tested."*
>
> **~ John Stevens, Budo Secrets**

I don't make promises lightly, but *I promise you this:* if you take these principles seriously, and diligently apply the lessons I have taught you in this book, they will radically change your life. The improvement will take time and effort, and for some it will be easier than for others, but I know unquestionably that every single person reading these words is capable of revolutionising their life.

Not everyone will do it. In fact, probably only a small minority will climb to the higher rungs of their full potential, but you are capable of great things. It is up to you to take responsibility for your own life, and discover what you will achieve.

> *"Out of every one hundred men, ten shouldn't even be there, eighty are just targets, nine are the real fighters, and we are lucky to have them, for they make the battle. Ah, but the one, one is a warrior, and he will bring the others back."*
>
> **~ Heraclitus**

道可道非常道
"Tao k'o Tao fei ch'ang Tao."
This is the very first line in Lao Tzu's ancient text; the Tao Te Ching.

Literally translated it reads, "Way named Way is not Way." However it can be more accurately understood as, "The Way which can be spoken of, is not the eternal Way."

This is probably the oldest recorded disclaimer in written history.

Lao Tzu included this as the very first line of his renowned text for an important reason. He wanted everyone to be very clear; to speak of the Way, is not to be confused with the Way itself.

> *"It is almost impossible to talk about Buddhism. So not to say anything, just to practice it, is the best way. Showing one finger or drawing a round circle may be the way, or simply to bow."*
>
> **~ Shunryu Suzuki**

Everything I have written in this book is inevitably meaningless, just words and text, black print on a white page. It is what you do with this information that gives it value.
The action you choose to take distinguishes you from others, and in the end, will tell the story of your life.

The deepest, most profound lessons you have yet to learn cannot be taught; they are beyond words and explanation. All each of us is able to do is live in accordance with the Way, and present our lives as testament to the depth of our understanding.

> *"Don't think, feel. It is like a finger pointing a way to the moon. Don't concentrate on the finger or you will miss all that heavenly glory."*
>
> **~ Bruce Lee**

- Three Rules
- Five Hindrances
- Daily Mantra
- Sixteen Virtues
- Memento Mori

Study the systems carefully, practice them diligently. With sufficient time and effort, you will reprogram your entire mode of being into something new, you will perish, disappear, and find yourself born again, living in accordance with the Martial Way.

FURTHER READING

Reading is underrated. Don't listen to anyone who tells you otherwise.

> *"The reading of all good books is like a conversation with the finest minds of past centuries."*
>
> **~ René Descartes**

I am not talking about reading news articles or blog posts, I mean a good book. Available to you now is a more extensive library of knowledge and wisdom than any other human being has ever had access to at any point in history. All this information at your very fingertips, you have but to reach out and take it!

> *"I cannot remember the books I've read any more than the meals I have eaten; even so, they have made me."*
>
> **~ Ralph Waldo Emerson**

I would never have come as far as I have were it not for the lessons of the great patriarchs and sages to have preceded me.

Here I will share with you a few of my most highly recommended books, so that you may deepen your understanding and expand your own realisation of the Way.

Meditations - Marcus Aurelius

If there is only one book you purchase on my recommendation, I beg you, let it be this. Never in my life have I ever read a more profound and applicable guide to life. Every household should have a copy of Marcus Aurelius' Meditations.

> *"Stoicism is an appropriate philosophy I would say, for serious, ruthless, introspective people, that want real answers and are willing to take no nonsense."*
>
> **~ Dr. Michael Sugrue**

The now widely practised Cognitive Behavioral Therapy is based heavily on the philosophy and practices of the great Stoic masters, illustrating that the lessons espoused by the great Roman Emperor Marcus Aurelius are as valid now as they were when they were first written, almost 2000 years ago.

I strongly recommend you purchase the Penguin Classics publication, with translation by Gregory Hays.

The Power of Now - Eckhart Tolle

I have read an extensive library of books related to meditation and mindfulness, and while I can recommend many great titles, each with their own merits, for the longest time I didn't have that single book I could recommend universally on the subject. At last I have that book, it is titled 'The Power of Now'.

This book is entirely non-denominational, it does not adhere to any one specific doctrine, but instead contains perennial wisdom and teachings from all the mainstream religions, non-theistic practices and scientific methods of mindfulness. The Power of Now will not give you any strict instruction on how to formally practice meditation, but the knowledge contained within is absolutely vital to the foundation of your practice, and your metaphysical understanding of reality.

Eckhart Tolle is one of the few truly awakened, contemporary teachers still living, and this book should be a cornerstone of your collection.

The Science of Enlightenment - Shinzen Young

Of the many teachers and sources of information I have learnt from, this book is one of the most influential in advancing me to my current practice of meditation.

Shinzen Young is an American who was ordained as a Shingon monk at Kōya-san, here in Japan. He is also a neuroscience research consultant, which gives a unique and powerful perspective to his work, which balances deeply spiritual insight with grounded, verifiable research.

I would describe this as a mid-level book, and not something I necessarily recommend to a beginner. But if you have some experience with meditation, it is a pivotal text which will add a lot of depth to your practice, and elevate you to the next level in your own journey.

The Way of Zen - Alan Watts

You are no doubt familiar with Alan Watts, or at least have heard the name. Many of his live recordings and radio lectures are available on YouTube, which are a delight to listen to, as he combines his rigid British boarding-school upbringing with his rock-and-roll persona and free thinking personality. Watts' work was crucial in popularising Eastern philosophy and spirituality in America and throughout the West during the late 50s and 60s.

If The Science of Enlightenment is important in my development of my current meditative practices, The Way of Zen is is absolutely critical in forming my philosophic understanding of Buddhism, Zen and the Tao. This book is simply astounding, and unrivaled in the manner it conveys the origins, meaning and interconnected nature of these three key Eastern philosophies. However, I must warn you, as accessible as Watts' recorded lectures are, this book is a little heavier, and much more academically written. Watts is a highly educated scholar, and this book lets you know it. Not recommended for beginners new to meditation and Zen, but absolutely indispensable for those seeking a true and complete understanding of the Way.

Letters from a Stoic - Seneca

When you have finished reading the great Marcus Aurelius' astounding work and are still desperate for more Stoicism, fear not, noble Lucilius Seneca has exactly what you need.

In contrast to the brief notes of Marcus' writing, Seneca wrote slightly more extensive lectures, which read much like a contemporary blog post or opinion piece. Seneca may not have the forthright brutality and military mind of Marcus, but what we lose in immediacy we gain in the beauty of prose. Seneca's letters are a delight to read, if reading Meditations is akin to a cold shower, Letters from a Stoic is the literary equivalent of bathing yourself in a piping-hot tub of scented oils.

Once again, I recommend the premier translation provided by the Penguin Classics publication.

***

This is the extent of the non-fiction text I recommend to you. However, I also have some fiction novels you may find enjoyable, which are educational from a more creative and entertaining perspective.

Learning does not always have to be dry and rigid. Throughout history we have always used stories, myths and legend to transmit and convey our most important lessons and highest ideals. You also need to take scheduled breaks and de-load your mind, to ease pressure and aid in recovery. This is the perfect time to pick up a good novel and enjoy an adventure, finely crafted for you by some of history's greatest storytellers.

Musashi - Yoshikawa Eiji

Musashi is the seminal samurai story.
This book (or series of books) provides a fictionalized account of the real life, legendary samurai, Miyamoto Musashi, who famously won over 60 duels and authored the acclaimed book *Go Rin No Sho*.

This novel was originally serialized in the newspaper Asahi Shimbun over a period of five years, it was then collated into a series of seven books, and is now available to purchase in one hardback copy. It is a fantastic story, a highly enjoyable tale of adventure and heroism in Japan's most romantic period. A classic tale of a wandering warrior who begins as a wild rogue, and is slowly honed into a master swordsman throughout his journey across the land.

Author Yoshikawa Eiji has a solid understanding of Musashi's philosophy and psychological approach to swordsmanship. I encourage you to enjoy this inspirational work of fiction as you rest and recover from your own training.

The Sound of Waves - Mishima Yukio

If you are unfamiliar with the name Mishima Yukio, take a break right now and do some research. Author, playwright, director, actor, model, very nationalistic, deeply conservative, wildly liberal, a little bit crazy and an absolute visionary. He is an amazing man who lived an incredible life, and is widely regarded as one of the most influential Japanese authors of the 20th century.

The Sound of Waves (潮騒 Shiosai) is not Mishima's most debated or highly celebrated work, but I recommend it to you now because it is a novel which perfectly represents Mishima's highest ideal. A story of a stoic man, even tempered, diligent, reserved, quietly passionate, supremely honourable, living a simple life, but a pure and honest one, this is Mishima's Übermensch.

The Sound of Waves is a shining beacon of wholesome values, its lead characters exemplars of traditional masculinity and femininity. I strongly recommend this fantastic novel for both men and women.

Gaunt's Ghosts - Dan Abnett

My last recommendation is a personal favourite that has grown with me over the last two decades. This series of sixteen books (plus spin-offs) is a military story set in a grim-dark science fiction world. Borrowing heavy influence from Bernard

Cornwell's Sharpe, it features a lot of action alongside extensive character development, as it explores the interconnected relationships and drama of the military unit as a whole.

I admit this series may not be to everyone's liking. Maybe I am taking liberties in sharing my own personal preferences. But I can assure you that Gaunt's Ghosts has played an influential role in my journey, especially in guiding me toward my own military experience, and the series enjoys a passionate place in my heart that I wish to share with you. For fans of science-fiction this is an oft-overlooked gem that you may just come to love.

Put the phone down and pick up a book.

Spend less time on social media, more time reading good literature. Carry a book with you when you go out, and make a habit of opening it up during those brief moments of down-time in which you would normally default to your phone. Check the screen time on your phone: how many hours a day do you spend with a phone in your hand? Imagine if you spent just half of that time reading, how many books you would have the pleasure to enjoy and learn from.

> *"No action should be undertaken without aim, or other than in conformity with a principle affirming the art of life."*
>
> **~ Marcus Aurelius**

Make reading great again.

THANK YOU FOR YOUR TIME AND EFFORT

This is not the beginning of your journey, nor is it the end. But I am honoured to join you here and walk alongside you for a short while.

> *"Do not think that*
> *This is all that exists*
> *There is much more to learn-*
> *The sword is unfathomable.*
> *The world is wide*
> *Full of happenings.*
> *Keep that in mind*
> *And never believe*
> *'I'm the only one who knows.'"*
>
> **~ Yamaoka Tesshu**

If you would like to support me and my work, I would greatly appreciate a positive rating and review online. Just a few moments of your time would mean more to me than you could possibly know.

I also want to hear about your thoughts and experience.
You can contact me directly on Twitter: @WayBudo
Or by email: budothemartialway@gmail.com
You can also find links to all of my content here:
https://budo.carrd.co
Feel free to contact me any time, I am here to work with you.

> *"I and Me are always too earnestly in conversation with one another: how could it be endured, if there were not a friend? For the hermit the friend is always the third person: the third person is the cork that prevents the conversation of the other two from sinking to the depths. Alas, for all hermits there are too many depths. That is why they long so much for a friend and for his heights."*
>
> **~ Friedrich Nietzsche**

Continue to walk the path, you are not alone. You are surrounded by countless brothers and sisters, ahead of you, behind you, and alongside you. We all wish to independently self-actualise, and become fully realised, sovereign individuals. But do not hesitate to find support from the sangha, the international community of warriors who strive on the same quest as you. We are in this together.

> *"I can do nothing for you but work on myself... you can do nothing for me but work on yourself."*
>
> **~ Ram Dass**

You know what to do. Remove distractions, abandon the old ways, and practice the systems and methods you have learnt. Those on the Way, become the Way.

~ Lewis E. Briggs

Made in the USA
Coppell, TX
07 January 2023

10635075R00066